This Book Is Shocking! Close Your Eyes When You Read It

D O M   S I L E O

PAGE PUBLISHING, INC.
Conneaut Lake, PA

First originally published by Page Publishing 2020

ISBN 978-1-64628-014-8 (pbk)
ISBN 978-1-66240-907-3 (hc)
ISBN 978-1-64628-015-5 (digital)

Printed in the United States of America

The Dedication

This book is dedicated to ALL the devoted people that buy, this book…
…and my wife

The Bill of Fare

Introduction

As the word chef of this book, I prepared a light buffet. On the menu, we have different dishes. We serve jokes sprinkled with mockery, with a side of nonsense. You pick and choose. Some dishes you will like, some you won't; some you'll go back to for a second helping. In other words, some like fish, some steak, and others are vegetarians. I hope you find something you like. On the menu, we have some stand-up routines, some jokes, some comic strips and cartoons, advice, and opinions. If you decide to stay, I say welcome!

But don't you hate it when somebody double parks, and there's an open car space right there, near the curb, just two feet away? OH! But that's another story… Has nothing to do with this book.

Book Titles

This Book Was Produced in a Facility That Contains Nuts.
Some Books Are Classics. This Is the Other One.
Nine-Fifths of All Books Are Nonsense.
Wagging Tales.
A Strange Tryst of Words
Great Literature Is Seldom Read. So Give This One A Try.
This Book Has Atrocious Morals…It Can Be Bought.
Damn! You look so GOOD holding, this book.
This Itsy-Bitsy Babel Is Available For Adoption.
If Trash Sells…You Could Be Holding a Bestseller!
Must Be Read at Room Temperature.
These Thoughts Are Extracted from an Abandoned Mind.
Truth Is Stranger Than Fiction…NOT Anymore!

Dom's Quotes

"When you Bury Fear—Miracles Grow."

"Good books and good wine shouldn't remain on the shelves."

"You don't move forward, trying to get back at someone."

"A good book is very easy on the ear."

"If your delusions are false to you, try mine."

"You'll NEVER get anything done, if you take everything into consideration."

"I attend church just to learn about sin."

"You don't have to be single, to be lonely."

"Politicians... For guys that are sinful, they PREY a lot."

"I was young once... Now, am muddle aged."

"People listen better... IF you agree with them."

"It's a PEACEFUL path, When the mind and the emotions come together."

"Vanity is My Favorite Motivator."

"Music is the Language of the GODS."

"Get rid of the virus of Bad thoughts...before They grow."

"95% of my life's pleasures, come from Anticipation."

Now...A helpful quote or line:

"Sorry! I don't remember your name...But, I remember, I liked you."

My Joke Journal

I could never bring myself to say the "N" word... I'm a married man, and I always have to say, "YES, dear. YES, dear."

You look perfect; go to the cemetery and see if they take walk-ins.

My old aunt died, and the funeral director was putting make-up on her... I said it won't help; she wasn't dating much before she died!

Do you think Smokey Robinson wants to be cremated?

I went to a fancy restaurant... They had VALET parking, and I feel so stupid... I brought a car.

The astrologer asked the politician, "What's your sign?"
He said, "For Sale."

Never bring a kazoo to the opera.

When you're old, you hate New Year's Eve... cause you just don't think ball dropping is any fun.

I was the principal dancer in "Death of a Salesman."

DOM SILEO

Did you hear about the pedophile who got all excited when he saw a Christmas sign that read, "Toys for Tots?"

The old lady said to her husband, "You know it's been a long time."
He said, "I don't think it could get hard."
She said, "I'm sure it's hard by now; it must be STALE!"

Question: Are Brazilian nuts…anything like a bikini wax?

My wife's not SKILLED at compliments. On our honeymoon, she said, "I had worst."

I have to be careful when I exercise. So I start slow, then I taper off.
I just get exhausted chasing the American dream.
I can do more jokes on exercise avoidance, but I don't want to push it.

A sign over a urinal: "Report all leaks to the management."

If the new toothpaste brightens your teeth in two weeks, in two months, you must glow in the dark.

The stewardess announcing, "There will be a slight delay, the Captain got on the wrong plane"

The Doctor says, to the patient "Your appendix is out… And while we were at it, We rotated your kidneys.

The cop pulled me over, and said "Didn't you see the Stop Sign?" I said "SURE, But, it didn't say where?"

Sign in vacant store: "Out of business since 1997"

My Joke Journal

I'm just catnip for the ladies. At the store, cashiers are always checking me out… and it's a fact, some of the ladies on line are after me.

A friend asked, "Could you talk your wife into a threesome?" I said, "I can't even talk her into a twosome."

My wife left high school twenty years ago, and she can still fit into the same earrings.

A friend asked me, "What's your secret for a long marriage?" I said, "Don't have a gun in the house."

Some guys have sweet flowery names for their spouses, like "Sweet pea" or "Buttercup"… All I could come up with was "The THORN!"

The wife says of our neighbor, "She always looks so CHEAP!" and the husband thinks, And you know how much, I love a bargain.

I went to the card store. I asked the clerk, "Do you have Valentine's cards for my beautiful wife?"
He said, "Sure, we have cards for ALL OCCASIONS!"
Then I said, "If you DO, do you have Valentine's cards for my beautiful… NEIGHBOR'S wife?"

Oh! She smells like a drunk… Oh! I like that in a woman.

I told my wife I feel like I'm out of the loop. She said, "Make a noose."

If you think dating was hard when you're younger, wait till you get married.

If it wasn't that I'm missing a few marbles, I'd be a complete idiot.

The wife says, "Do you love me?"
I say, "Of course."
She says, "Prove it."
I always say, "Yes! You look THIN—without laughing."

It's sad when you get old. Today, when I see a beautiful girl go by, I can only get a lump in my throat.

Is artificial respiration just another word for faking it?

I got a new book out; it's called Stupidity for Dummies.

The wife asked, "We're going out tonight. Do you KNOW what you're gonna wear?"
I say "Sure; whatever I eat!"

My wife demands, she wants jewelry for her birthday… So, I go to the jeweler and ask him "Do you have anything with a curse on it?"

You don't have to remove your shoes and socks, If the door-mat says "Wipe your feet."

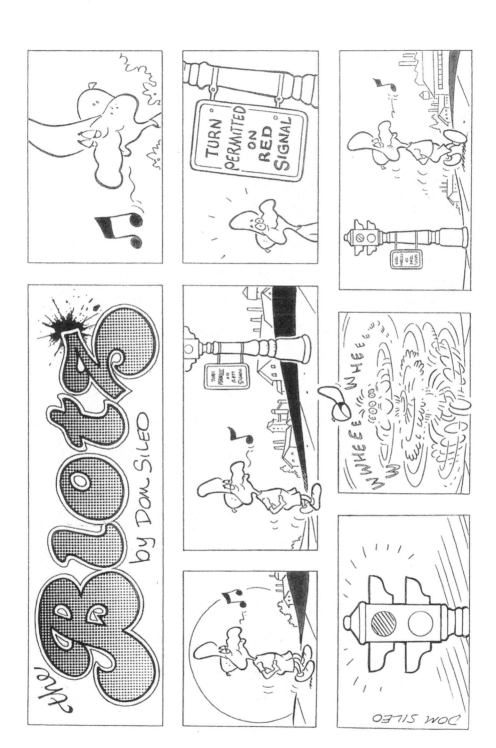

The Blotz

The Blotz's dog Dudley

The Children's Dance Recital

"Damn!" Time runs on the EXPRESS track when you get older…But…Here's my little secret for slowing down time. Just attend a Children's Dance Recital! Last week, I went to my granddaughter's dance recital. Her Dance was number 27. At dance number 11, I began, to slowly slip into a COMA…as time, careened off the rails and suddenly died!! Sixteen more dances at five minutes a dance… Just SHOOT ME!

Around dance number 15, the wife says to me, "I can't hear the music; your stomach's GROWLING so loud." I say, "Er…Since I've been here, my stomach thinks I'm on a HUNGER-STRIKE. I'm gonna call and have a pizza delivered HERE. Do you want anything?" The wife says, "Yep! A little slice of SILENCE!" Then I say, "I'll call 911, and say, 'There's a man sitting in the dark, looking at LITTLE girls. Come and get him!" Then the wife says, "And make sure they bring a STRAITJACKET in your size!" Then the wife says, "OKAY! Who are you calling now?" I tell her, "The Suicide Hotline," and the wife says, "Suicide! Don't bother! You don't SHUT that phone, I'm gonna KILL you!" I tell the wife, "Relax, I'm half dead now. If they could BOTTLE a Kids' Dance Recital, they'll have the cure for INSOMNIA!"

Dance number 19 on the program is "Swan Lake." On the stage, it looks like "Lost in Space." The next dance, a group of "Gravity-Enhanced" kids do "The Dance Of The Sugar PLUMPED Fairies." The next dance up, I can't find on my program so I'll just call it, "Kids LOITERING on stage, with Music."

Dance number 24, former students come out and do a thing called "Beyond Dance." This is Beyond Torture. Ouch! YOWEE! They should've titled this dance recital "To INFINITY and BEYOND" Just then, the wife says, "Stop fidgeting!" I say, "I can't help it; my seat is broken. OUCH! And it's breaking my back." Then the wife says, "Well, thank God, your stomach stopped GROWLING." I say, "That's because I ATE the flowers we brought for the kid."

Finally, it's over, and we take a picture. There's my granddaughter crying with a bouquet of STEMS; and me, I'm smiling like I just passed a STONE.

"the Muttermans"

"Morty"

MORTY IS AFRAID TO TALK BACK TO HIS WIFE...
SO, HE MUTTERS, UNDER HIS BREATHE.
SHE TELLS HIM "NO" ALL THE TIME.
HE TOLD HER, "NO" ONCE... BUT, HAS
SINCE, LEARNED HIS LESSON.

"Inez"

HOW DO YOU KEEP A FAMILY TOGETHER,
WHEN EVERYONE'S GROWING AT DIFFERENT
RATES & GOING IN DIFFERENT DIRECTIONS?
THANK GOD MORTY'S STAGNANT. ER..
DON'T TELL MORTY I SAID THAT.

HOLLY the LOOPY SURREAL DAUGHTER

BUSTER a FLIP, WISE-CRACKING SON

"Peeves"

... IS THEIR MILITANT PET DOG (WHO FEELS HE'S A CAT
IN A DOGS BODY) & HE WANTS EQUAL RIGHTS WITH CATS

HEY! WHAT AM I DOING AT THE BOTTOM OF THIS PAGE?

THIS WOULD NEVER HAPPEN TO A CAT!

The MUTTERMANS

The MUTTERMANS

The MUTTERMANS

The MUTTERMANS

The MUTTERMANS

The Muttermans daughter Holly

The MUTTERMANS

LOST YOUR KEYS AGAIN!!

SHE THINKS SHE'S SO SMART... I'M NOT GONNA ANSWER HER.

AND WHEN I FIND MY KEYS, I'M NOT EVEN GONNA ASK WHERE I PARKED THE CAR.

The MUTTERMANS

WHY CAN'T I COMPLAIN ABOUT SOMETHING WITHOUT YOU SAYING..."OH IT AIN'T THAT BAD"?

CAUSE IT AIN'T THAT BAD

OF COURSE IT'S NOT THAT BAD, THE INJURY IS MINE, BUT IF IT WAS YOURS, LOOK OUT!

I'M SORRY WE DISAGREE ON SOME THINGS!

SOME'THINGS'?

I'M NOT EVEN GOING TO MENTION WHO HAS TO HAVE THE LAST WORD

DON'T GO THERE

The MUTTERMANS

HERE'S SOME GREAT ADVICE – A MAN NEVER GETS MAD AT HIS WIFE IF SHE YELLS AND SCREAMS AT HIM.

HE ONLY GETS MAD IF HE LISTENS.

MORT!!

HE GAVE THAT ADVICE IN A GUTSY VOICE... PITY! HIS FEET DIDN'T HEAR IT!

Wilbur

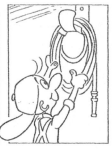

Great Art vs. Abstract Art

Great art, like great music, just pulls you in, and for a brief moment, you soar. As you escape the imprisonment of your mind and body, you feel the connection; you feel the magic. You question, "How does he do that?" You can't explain it. It's just like being in love.

But abstract art comes with a story; it has to be explained (the provenance/ancestry) and the longer the explanation, the more odorous the art. It's not about liking the childlike art; it's about the buying and selling. So to secure their investments, both sellers and buyers have to talk up this so-called art.

In abstract art, they reimagine, reinterpret and reject traditional values, with no restrictions, no criteria, and no standards. But in real art, you must have standards...You have to DRAW the line some place. In baseball, you hit a ball over the foul line, it's called a FOUL...In abstract art, they will call that a HOME RUN! Listen, calling a foul ball a home run doesn't make it so.

Not every baseball player hits home runs time after time. But every Picasso is a home run. Every single Picasso is "A Picasso." How come you can't tell which Picasso is better than the others? (They say "Don't go to a plastic surgeon, If he has a Picasso painting hanging on his wall.") In the Walter Foster art book number 97, *Painting and Mixing Colors*, Picasso admits he's not a great artist: "I'm one who understood his times, and has exhausted, as best he could, the imbecility of his contemporaries."

Speaking of great promoters, in Hans Christian Anderson's story, "The Emperor's New Clothes," the two swindler tailors tell the Emperor their clothes are invisible to anyone that's STUPID! That's like saying abstract art is really great art; if you can't see it, you're stupid. We (the promoters) know better than you. Listen, if we accept the lying in promoting abstract art, the next thing you know, they'll be lying in politics.

"Girl B4 a MIRROR" by Pablum Picasso

Guesstimating Advice

(For my grandkids)

People are always giving advice; the question is, how do you know the good advice from the bad? Certainly, bad advice is worse than no advice at all. So here are some of my ideas, so you can judge. (Of course, you can certainly add your own ideas as well.) First question in all advice, ask yourself: does this make sense? Does it feel right, or do you still have doubts? Does this make the problem clearer? If I follow this advice, would I have a successful result? What if I do the opposite of this advice? What if I did nothing at all?

Bad advice can come from anybody and any source. Remember, the source of the advice is less important than the advice itself...Even when the advice comes from YouTube, a book, esteemed teacher, a PhD, even from a loving grandpa. Like they say, "Never ask a barber if you need a haircut." Don't buy the guy (He's so nice.), buy the advice. If someone gave you a sweater that didn't fit, you'd return it. Good advice measures up...

(Now this, try to increase your capacity for happiness. When you're MAD at somebody, chances are you're mad at yourself. Try to decrease your capacity for getting annoyed, at yourself or anybody else. This doesn't accomplish anything.) When someone does something idiotic, don't stamp your feet and pout. There's no honor, in out-performing an idiot! It's your choice, a life of love or hate. You alone pack the emotional baggage for your trip through life. That's just my advice, and I would be proud...if you questioned it.

Giblets

Ruppert T. Giblets...

RUPPERT IS A GUY, JUST TRYING TO GET THROUGH THE DAY. HE FEELS "NO NEWS IS GOOD NEWS." ... SO, HE NEVER READS A NEWSPAPER ... NEVER HAS TURNED ON A RADIO or TV.

HE HAS TWO ASSOCIATES, ONE IS NAMED KAZOU (AN INDIAN) & DUDLEY (HIS DOG)

Zelda ...

SEES VALUE IN DISCARDED ODDS and ENDS. SO, SHE'S SO HAPPY TO BE MARRIED TO RUPPERT. "IT TAKES GUTS TO BE A GIBLET." SHE SAYS "I'M ALSO HAPPY... CAUSE THIS IS THE FIRST TIME, I'M IN A COMIC STRIP."

Okay!... Let's Party!!

Giblets

First appearance of "Giblets"..Later, to be revised)

I included these "giblets" strips cause my son, Frank (age 14) gave me the fish joke.

GIBLETS

GIBLETS

GIBLETS

GIBLETS

GIBLETS

GIBLETS

GIBLETS

GIBLETS

"OOOOOH!… I HOPE I DIDN'T FORGET ANYTHING!!!"

The Soulmate Compass

Isn't it AMAZING, you can find your one true love ONLY in your own hometown? Of course, you're not gonna fall in love with someone who's NOT there. Strange how people in Pennsylvania find their one TRUE love only in Pennsylvania. People in the other fifty states do the same thing. The point being, there isn't only ONE true love, and thank God! Because if that was TRUE, then your chances of finding your ONE true love would be ONE in a little more then three hundred million people (That's the USA population).

That being said: Here are some guidelines on how to pick a mate.

Some people are easier to love than others. Find that person. BE that person.

Easy-to-love people love many things, and they love life!

Hard-to-love people hate many things; they hate themselves and hate their lives! Why would you want to hang out with them?

Someone who smiles is easy to love. We love people who are happy to see us. Someone who doesn't smile comes with too much baggage, and it's a heavy lift (It's just too much work to make them smile). NEVER marry someone with MORE problems than you!

Does this person diminish you or increase you? Help you to fulfill your Dreams? Do you feel happy in their presence, or do you feel unworthy and uneasy?

There's a ratio between JOY and AGGRAVATION; let the scales tip in favor of joy. If not, just leave. Who needs this?

Plus, if you choose the WRONG person for yourself, you've just put-up a roadblock to the RIGHT person for yourself... DON'T put up roadblocks to happiness!

The smartest thing you can do is to make yourself happy. So you'll want to pick someone who will help you achieve that goal.

People are always good company, IF they WANT to be there, whether it's marriage or a job. The WORST marriages and jobs are the ones you don't want to be in.

Here's two questions to help you decide IF this Person's "The ONE":

1. IF you won $100,000,000 lottery, would you still be with this person?
2. IF this person was gone from your life, would you be SAD or ELATED?

When you think of a mate, trust your FEELINGS; feelings don't LIE. Have you ever looked at a kitten, a puppy, or a baby? The corners of your mouth turn up. If you're with someone you love, the corners of your mouth will go up; you just can't help it. If the corners don't go up, DON'T marry. Now, if you like someone, ask them out. If they say NO, It will be painful, for a short while; but if you missed the opportunity, you may have regrets that'll last a LIFETIME! Regrets last longer than rejections (Regrets can be a b– – –h!).

Listen, you didn't pick your friends for their sex appeal, but find the traits you like in your friends: a sense of humor, intelligence, sports, theater, music, art, etc...Now transfer that to your future partner. If she/he has all the traits you love, PLUS the sex appeal, you've hit a home run! It's connection versus misconnection! The more you like the same things, the stronger the connection.

When it comes to marriage, if you have to ask someone else if you should marry this person, don't marry! The ONLY person to answer that question is YOU! Making your own decisions is EMPOWERING…try it.

When you say YES, you must feel like the stars are aligned! That the Gods are smiling, and all is right with the world! Select. DON'T settle. If you like oranges, don't marry a kumquat! People have done this, but you can't get orange juice from an kumquat!

This is the time to think about yourself! When you stick up for yourself, you'd be SURPRISED how many things work out in your favor.

If a person says, "I love you," great! But now ask that person to define love. People have different definitions of what love is. You have to be on the same page. Some People really DON'T know what love is. They really don't. You spend time with the things you love… Some people say, "I married you! See, that proves I love you! Now leave me alone! I want to spend, ALL my free time with my friends!"

These poor people were brought up in dysfunctional homes. As Ron White says, "You can't fix STUPID!" Don't marry stupid. That would be stupid!

"IT MAY LOOK LIKE A SILLY COVERED POOL NOW…BUT
COMES THE WARM WEATHER AND I'M ON MY BOAT"

"I ALWAYS SAY YOU'VE GOT TO TRAVEL
TO MEET THE RIGHT PEOPLE"

THIS BOOK IS SHOCKING! | 39

Stand-Up Advice

Never get on stage if you don't feel like it. Your job is to bring the passion and fun to the stage. The dusty stage doesn't bring the passion to you. People are always good company, if they want to be there. People mirror you. Chris Rock said, "If your embarrassed on stage, the audience is gonna be embarrassed for you." People are in touch with their emotions, more than their intellect. You connect emotionally. Be in the moment; that means, "Be on the stage, not on the page." If your trying to remember every comma and the correct word order of a joke that's written on the page, your mind is on the page, NOT on the stage. You have to be present to make the connection with the audience.

If you get nervous before a performance, slow down. Going fast can make you anxious. The quicker you talk, the more anxious you sound. Jokes are set-up and punchline. If you rush when you talk, the audience doesn't have time to absorb the set-up or even hear it. Keep the mic next to your chin, so they can hear you. Always pause before a punchline, that's the audience's cue to get ready to laugh. Don't step on the punchline; let it breathe.

Going slow creates tension, which will be (hopefully) relieved by the punchline. Going slow looks like you're in control. New guys go much too fast. They're, maybe, scared and want to get it over with. Take the mask off when you perform. Don't hold back (If you're scared or emotional, tell the audience). If you hold back, that'll put up a barrier between you and the audience. Barriers (mask) don't make you connect with the audience. The truth must come without excuses or barriers, if you want to connect.

Practice makes perfect, but only if you practice perfectly. If you practice sloppily, you'll be practicing mistakes. Onstage, don't be afraid to make a mistake. It'll be honest, and when you laugh at yourself, they'll laugh with you. The fear of bombing is worse than the bombing. Plus, if you're lucky, when you bomb, you'll realize what NOT to do the next time.

You can't tell if an audience is gonna be receptive to a joke. There are some who like steak, who likes fish, who's a vegetarian; we all have different taste. Plus, when you tell your best joke, the guy in the audience is maybe thinking, Did I leave the lights on in the car? So you try the joke a few more times with a different audience and see how it goes. Trying to figure what different people want and trying to slant your jokes for all tastes is not only impossible, but you'll lose yourself. So you have to make sure you like the jokes. I try to make myself smile. Plus, if I like a joke, I can better sell it. When I tell a joke that doesn't go over, I think that's another jewel in the crown and I laugh to myself cause I want to have fun in life, as well as onstage.

Open Mic

(Where You Practice Your Stand-Up Act and You Don't Get Paid)

Hello, how are you? Hello...Now, I didn't write that particular greeting, "Hello, how are you?" I STOLE it. I hope you can forgive me, you judgmental jealous bastards. Now, it's really a THRILL to be here. I'm really excited to be here cause I'm coming to you almost LIVE (I'm a grandpa), and it's not only a big thrill to be here, it's also a big, INCONVENIENCE. A three-hour round trip to do a LOUSY five minutes! There's an actual clinical term for people who do this. It's called "CRAZY BASTARDS." That being said, I do three different comic routines: the one I practiced, the one I do, and the one I WISHED I did! But you know, it's a SAD day when you're at an open mic and you suddenly realize that you're at the PEAK of your earning power... and that's why I buy LOTTO tickets... It's NOT that I'm addicted to gambling; it's just that I'm addicted to DISAPPOINTMENT, and that's the real reason I started doing, stand-up. And thank you, for feeding THAT addiction.

(One PATHETIC laugh is fine; my laughs ain't used to crowds.)

You know, the LAST time I performed, I got a standing BOOvation, but NOT like today—I never seen such an awesome INDIFFERENCE. Oh, by the way, all the MONEY I make here tonight is going to CHARITY.

You know, they say old habits die HARD; for me, they died SOFT.

The other day, I just step out of the bathroom and the wife says, "Hey! Your fly's open."

I tell her, "Hey! You don't have to LOCK the cage when the canary's dead."

When I cracked that joke, a girl in the audience was so sympathetic, she said, "Sorry."

I said "NO hard feelings."

But, the WIFE is so sympathetic, so compassionate, she says things like, "Is that a TIC TAC in your pocket, or are you just HAPPY to see me?"

Okay! This next BIT, I call little CRAZIES.

Ladies, the "REAL" reason men pee all over the TOILET is simply because our aim is COCK-EYED and my thinking maybe cock-eyed, but I think all SEX TOY, manufacturers are JEWISH; you ever see a vibrator that wasn't CIRCUMCISED?

(Speaking about RELIGION)

I think GOD loved the gays cause when GOD, gave man the ninth commandment, it said, "Thou shall not COVET thy neighbor's wife."

So obviously, the neighbor's husband's up for GRABS.

Today, there should be an eleventh commandment, condemning talk radio; it's so partisan, so DIVISIVE and NASTY!

And why can't we all just get along? Cause if you go back FAR enough, you'll see we're all RELATED. In fact, we ALL had the same LAST name; I checked. You've got your Jew bastards, Black bastards, Guinea bastards, Liberal bastards, Conservative bastards; there's the skinny bastards and fat bastards, and then there's those RICH bastards, and we all feel sorry for those POOR bastards; and there's the ever present DUMB bastards; and let's not forget those CRAZY bastards, you see them all over the place—most of US are doing stand-up.

Speaking of comedians, I think other comedians, love me more than my wife. She's FRIGID and doesn't ever care if I ever GET OFF; other comedians can't wait!

Well, I can see my time is almost up. Thank you, for feeding my disappointment ADDICTION. By saving some of MY LAUGHS for the NEXT act.

But before I go, I want to say NY is the GREATEST city in the world. It's a city that never sleeps, EXCEPT in places where people see my act. God bless America; Support OUR troops and you're STILL the BEST crowd I've ever seen. Give yourselves a hand and I'll PRETEND it's for me.

(If you want to do an open mic in your city, go to www.badslava.com)

Macy's

Let me tell you, nothing—NOTHING—cries and screams, EXCITEMENT like saying, "I'm a married man."

Okay, so I'm sitting in my E-Z chair trying to forget that reality, when I hear the wife say, "Hey, Dom! I just got some Macy's COUPONS…"

And I say, "Oh, God! And I just got some CHEST pains," and she says, "With ALL these coupons, I get 20 to 30 percent OFF."

And I say, "YOU'VE got to be 100 percent OFF if you THINK I'm going with you."

And she says, "I need SHOES, BLOUSES, PANTS…"

And I say, "You're also gonna need a GUN! if you think I'm going with you." Of course, I said ALL that stuff on the INSIDE cause I don't want to cause any TROUBLE.

And before I can even, say, "YES, DEAR. Yes, dear," we're at MACY'S, and she's grabbing THIS, THAT, and the OTHER thing, off the racks, and we head toward the FITTING rooms. We pass three guys with glazed over EYES sitting down with WOMEN'S pocket-books on their LAPS, looking like ZOMBIES. I quickly recognize that species as "THE MARRIED MAN." Sometimes, at MACY'S, you see a young guy following his girlfriend around, looking like a FREAKING Zombie; he's a "Married Man in TRAINING!"

I quickly turn to face the wife, and she throws her PURSE at me and says, "Dom! Sit DOWN on that couch and keep an eye on my bag!"

I say, "NO!" She throws me a LOOK, and I say, "I prefer to STAND. I prefer to stand," and she goes into the FITTING room.

Now, not only am I annoyed, I'm also EMBARRASSED. I mean, her bag doesn't even MATCH my shoes! So I quietly join the other zombies on the "COUCH of the LIVING DEAD."

So I'm sitting there, half-asleep, and my eyes start to GLAZE over, and I start getting some zombie thoughts: What if Aladdin Opened a FUNERAL home? Would he call it ABRA-CADAVER? And you know, when you go to a funeral home, and you VIEW the body, they call that A WAKE. Hey, if that's awake, I HATE to see what they call ASLEEP! And the next day, you read the obituary, it says, "the LATE Mr. Katz." I say, forget "the late;" this guy ain't NEVER showing-up. And how do you throw a SURPRISE birthday party for a PSYCHIC? What the hell is DRACULA'S first name? My mind's wandering all over the place, but not this EYE; it's staying focused right on HER bag!

Just then, one of the DEAD guys pokes me and says, "Thank God, this will all be over soon."

I say, "Wah?"

The DEAD guy continues, "My wife has a nail appointment, and once her nails are done, she can't do anything. Can't open her purse, can't fumble for her keys; it'll RUIN her nails. I even have to light her CIGARS..."

And I'm thinking, Who's gonna WIPE her ass?

But I don't tell that to the zombie! I tell him, "Hey! What the hell is it with the nails anyway? I mean, what's the FIRST thing a guy says when he sees a girl, 'WOW! Look at the SET of nails on that broad' (cause we're VERY interested in the nails.)?

"You know, sometimes, the wife catches me looking at a pretty GIRL, and she says, 'What the hell are you looking at?' I say, 'The NAILS. The nails.'"

Just then, the MOST pretentious woman walks by with the LONGEST nails you ever saw, all ACRYLIC and rhinestones. Like she's the TOTAL package: never mind that FAT ASS, those nails are gonna clinch the deal! You ever notice, the bigger the ASS, the longer the NAILS?

The Dead-Guy says, "Those nails...it's like polishing the HOOVES of a cow."

I say, "UDDER-LY ridiculous."

The Dead-guy chuckles and says, "Don't milk it" (We're bonding), and then he says, "BUT did you notice she had a nice set of gazongas?"

I say, "Did I NOTICE? They were RIGHT out there; you couldn't help but NOTICE!"

But HEY! I don't feel GUILTY. It's NOT that I looked at them with TWO eyes; ONE eye always stayed focused on my wife's BAG!

Just then the wife comes out of the fitting room, and now, the INTERROGATION starts, "How does THIS look? How does THAT look?"

I once made a mistake; I said, "I DON'T like it."

She said, "What do you know?"

And I said, "So why the HELL, do you ask me?"

But she continues to ASK, and now, I just smile and nod. After a while, she says, "Nothing looks right...Let's go! Give me my bag! I want to phone for a NAIL appointment." Then, she says, "Oh, wait! I just found Discount Coupons in my bag for the SHOE Factory!"

DAMN! I should have looked in her BAG! Then, she repeats those TWO words: "Let's GO."

Immediately, TWO words pop into my head THAT I'd like to repeat... It's "Thank you! Thank you!"

"SOB" the LAST TIME I SAW HIM, HE
WAS TAKING A <u>HOT</u> SHOWER"

"TERMITES!!"

"YOU WANT OUR REPORT ON BRIBES… IT'LL COST YOU!!"

"...AND THEN AFTER I SEE MYSELF BEING WITTY ON THE TONIGHT SHOW... I GET A SHOW OF..."

Marriage

WOW! What a good looking crowd. What a good looking crowd.

I really mean it… It's TRUE… It's true. Individually, not so much…But as a group, thumbs up. Aside from that, I hope you're all feeling great because I'm feeling great; my AUTOPSY came back NEGATIVE.

The doctor said he's sorry about the autopsy, but I should have told him I was MARRIED MAN.

Talking about marriage…I'm glad the wife never threw out her wedding gown because if anything goes wrong, I still got the ORIGINAL PACKAGING…and what could go wrong?

Well, it started years ago, when we honeymooned at Disney and every night we went to bed, she would lift up the covers and start to sing, "It's a SMALL WORLD after all, it's a small world after all…" I hate that song, I hate that song!

But I don't want to COMPLAIN! But, I can never forget those fights… She called me a LOUSY lover… A lousy lover. She said, "You finished in LESS than three minutes!" I said, "I'm a lousy lover? You're the goddamn PROCRASTINATOR!" But honestly, I think I lasted three and a half minutes.

But I didn't argue because that three and a half minutes took a lot out of me. But the fights continued anyway!

She said, "That was very nasty; you calling me a procrastinator!"

Then I said, "OH! That was very sweet; you calling me "GREASED LIGHTNIN'!"

And it's NOT like we couldn't end the fights, it's just that we're trying to AVOID that MAKE-UP sex.

But I don't want to COMPLAIN! But we have different likes and dislikes: she likes it in the FRONT; I like it in the BACK. So one time, I rented a room in a very HIGH-CLASS hotel, right across the street from The Waldorf, and even before we unpacked, she ran..., right into the bathroom and said, "See! The toilet paper HANGS in the FRONT, not the BACK, you PUTZ!" She called me a putz. Oh! That's so charming; right across the street from The Waldorf!

But you know, sometimes she can be quite loving. I think she's BI-POLISH and those loving times, I call her my Little Volcano of Love.

Er... I call her the little volcano because she's SHORT. I mean, she can walk under a CHIHUAHUA without pushing his BALLS to the SIDE. (Her sister, on the other hand, the balls would HIT her right in the face! Because she's the TALL one.)

Oh, yeah! Back to last week. Now, the wife brought a pair of BLACK LACE panties. OKAY, okay...Now, black lace panties are very, VERY SEXY... But NOT over a pair DEPENDS.

Now, these things don't help me with my problems. You see my COLD water PIPE is working fine; it's my HOT water pipe that's giving me trouble.

So I went to the doctor and told him there's NO starch in my HOT water pipe; I can't get it HARD even, if I put it in the FREEZER. The doctor said, "No problem. I got just the thing for you, 'CIALIS'"

I said, "GREAT! Just don't tell my wife about...ALICE!"

I joke around all the time and it annoys the hell out of the wife. Maybe that's why I do it. Like the other day, we're in a restaurant, and the waiter said, "Sir, your meal comes with a salad. Would you like a salad on the side?"

DOM SILEO

I said, "No. I like a salad IN a plate…CATHERINE ZETA JONES, on the SIDE."

Later, the wife said, "Dom, will you stop with your stupid jokes? Your jokes are like our SEX LIFE, the only difference is now, my embarrassment is in PUBLIC."

I start to object but say nothing because with age comes WISDOM and I got a lot of wisdom. It's TRUE, it's true. Of course, I can't find it when I NEED it, but I Got it.

In INDIA, they look for wisdom in MEDITATION. In my house, we call that a NAP! But in my house, you only take SHORT naps because if you take a LONG nap, they start looking for the WILL.

Now, in my will, I instructed my daughter to do my EUOLGY and then the wife said, "Oh, that's GREAT! Then I'll do the REBUTTAL!" (She always has to have the last word.)

And before my last word, I just want to say I love doing stand-up; it's a lot of FUN. But at my age, when I see the LIGHT, and I hear, "That's your time," I just hope it's NOT God talking.

Religion

Hello. Now, I pray this goes well, But I'm not too sure that it will, because I'm an AGNOSTIC. Okay, when the church says, "It's better to give, than to receive," then they send me DONATION envelopes, I DON'T return them!

Okay. So I once had a DREAM that ALL, the world's holiest religious leaders came together for an intense…coitus…CAUCUS…Okay, just a meeting! And after MUCH talk, they finally reached this very "remarkable AGREEMENT." They ALL agreed THAT the other guys' religion is BULLSHIT!

Then, BOOM! GOD suddenly appeared and he said, "Oh my ME! What PRETENTIOUS righteousness! Who do they think THEY are? Our Honorable and Dee-STINK-guished politicians?"

Just then, an ATHEIST asked GOD, "Why do religions always start wars, then pray for peace?"

And GOD said, "See? Right there! This is the height of BULLSHIT! An ATHEIST asking ME a question."

MY favorite bible Story is when God FORBADE Adam and Eve to eat from the "TREE of Knowledge," but from the "Tree of STUPIDITY." Bon Appétit!

That's why I'm a "Born Again Agnostic." But my dog's an atheist; he stopped believing in GOD when I had him DEBALLED!

Speaking of Death, there may be a little truth to LIFE after DEATH because I witnessed, with my own eyes, when my neighbor DIED, almost immediately, his wife came back to life!

DOM SILEO

Okay, back to the Bible. It says in the Bible, "GOD made man in his image." WOW! So God looks like ME! Then, I guess, circumcision is just TWEAKING God's image!

Speaking of CIRCUMCISIONS, if a man thinks with his dick, you've just given him a FRONTAL LOBOTOMY!

Speaking of "Lobotomies," a friend YELLED at me, he said, "You should NEVER make fun of religion!" Then, much later, after much careful THOUGHT and consideration, I went to church and BLEW OUT a candle in his name.

People say they CHOOSE their own religion. Bullshit! You were BORN into it! Like you're born in BOSTON and your favorite team is the YANKEES!! Hey! Worshippers, you never did "CHOOSE." Look! If you really gave a kid a CHOICE, he'd pick DISNEY!

One day, I'd like to start, my own TV religion. I'd call it, "The MINISTRY of GUILT." Curbing everyone's enthusiasm, I'll turn a satellite DISH into a collection PLATE. So to reserve your room in HEAVEN, with BEST views, just simply, send ME your money and riches "NOW!" And your RICHES will come when you're DEAD! And Remember, my MINISTRY is the only ONE that comes with a money-back GUARANTEE. If you're NOT in Heaven two weeks after you're DEAD, just WALK into my office for a FULL refund!

Okay, now, it's strange, How God works in MYSTERIOUS ways. When I was younger, I was always comfortable going to church, and that comfort turned into RAPTURE—when the SERVICE was over!

The last time I felt RAPTURE like this, I was at Disney!

DOM SILEO

"NOW WHERE'D EGO?"

"SURE! I TEACH MY CHILDREN TO
SHARE...BUT...BUT...BUT..."

"EURIPIDES TYPED??!"

It's Sweet to Do Nothing

Okay, it's GOOD to be here. It's really good to be here. SO, right away, you can tell how EASILY pleased I am! Easily PLEASED, that's ME. Because STRESS and strain are NOT my cup of COFFEE! Now I'll tell you, when you get older, you start to get lazy, and that could be real trouble for me because I started out lazy. Now, you may think that I don't do anything, BUT time is PRECIOUS and we mustn't WASTE it—NEVER waste it! And even if I ONLY have just a few minutes to kill, I take a NAP! Oh, a nap! That's my SIGNATURE move! And sometimes, I dream I'm a movie EXTRA who becomes a MAJOR star by sleeping his way to the TOP!

A friend asked me, "When you do stand-up, do you have DOUBTS?" HEY! I have doubts when I get out of BED! But the truth is I was hoping I'd get so GOOD at this that I could do it in my SLEEP! Oh! Oh! I can see that some of you are so good at listening that you're starting to go to sleep on me. But That's okay because I'll just consider that a "HIBERNATING Standing Ovation!" Please, don't get up; remain in your STOOLS!

Okay. So I like watching TV. I like getting a HAIRCUT. I like riding in an ESCALATOR because I'm doing something and doing NOTHING at the same time. Oh! "It's so sweet to do nothing."

I once belonged to a club I called "It's Sweet to Do NOTHING." The official name was "Workaholics Anonymous." Our club SLOGAN was "Don't WAIT; Procrastinate NOW!" Of course, we always have trouble starting meetings. But our CLUB president was always there. He's HOMELESS!

So I'm at home, lying down on the couch, and the wife yelled at me, "GET UP!"

I told her, "HEY! I'm doing CLUB WORK." Then, she said "Okay! You've done enough CLUB work! Let's go on VACATION!" I said, "But, a NAP is the perfect vacation." Then, she said, "Let's go to ASIA." Then I said, "If I wanted to MEET Foreigners, I'd go visit my doctors!" The wife said, "I'll call the airlines." I said, "STOP! You know what the MOTTO of the airlines is? They say, 'IF we treated everybody EQUALLY, then FIRST class wouldn't be so SPECIAL. So we have to treat the economy people, like SHIT!'" Then, the wife said, "Then let's take a CRUISE. I can't wait to see all the SIGHTS!"

Talk about SIGHTS, we were once on a cruise ship, in a very small cabin. NO windows, but every time I stepped out of the SHOWER, there was a MIRROR! Oh! That's NOT a pretty SIGHT! But the wife said, "Putz! Getting there is half the FUN." Then I said, "Then coming BACK should be ALL the fun; why GO? I'm already HERE!" Then, I turned and looked at the wife and she's starting to get MAD. Then the wife said, "OKAY, Mr. Cadaver. Then, we'll just SIT home and do nothing."

Then, I teased her and I said, "Au Contraire, HONEY LUMP! I'm Not SITTING here doing nothing. I'm LAYING down here, THINKING of ways to make us RICH! "I called the HOME SHOPPING network and gave them a few of my ideas:

> Number 1: a LINE of beautiful designed, com-
> memorative, PAPER plates for home-
> less people. So they can DECORATE
> their CARDBOARD boxes;
> Number 2: For OVERWEIGHT people that
> give-up too easily, "EDIBLE DIET books;"
> Number 3: For lost and confused people,
> BIBLES with GPSs. So they can GET
> GUIDANCE from above…"

Speaking of religion, I once belonged to a very silent "Religious CULT." The silence was so SEVERE that our church services were performed by a group of DERANGED MIMES!

But I had to leave that CULT because, I HATE any religion that preaches lead us NOT into Temptation. I say, LEAD me! Lead me! I was once "TEMPTED" to write my congressman, in Washington, C.D. and say, "I think The Seven Deadly Sins should be INCLUDED in the Bill of Rights." I think the church condemns the pleasures in life just to make them more fun.

You know, I once witnessed a marriage ceremony performed in the "CHAPEL OF TRUTH." The Pastor said, "I now pronounce you MAN and PAIN in the ASS (because it was the "CHAPEL OF TRUTH!")"

Hey! That's ONLY a joke! The wife doesn't mind that joke. She's very cool and SUPPORTIVE. How supportive is she? She's so supportive, I once heard, her on her phone, she called that "Make a WISH Foundation" and she asked them, "Could you, please, just kill my husband?" See, THAT was a joke too! The truth is the wife is very SUPPORTIVE. When I left home to come here, she gave me some very inspirational words THAT I must never, NEVER forget. She said, "Dom, we need bread."

And now, to get a bit serious because ALL those LAUGHS are throwing off my timing. They say "A thing of BEAUTY is a JOY Forever," but NOT if it's a CHEESECAKE. That's evil. Pssst. It calls you in the middle of the night. It says, "One slice, can't hurt." That's devil work.

Okay, IF it's TRUE that the older you get the WISER you get, so How come old men always look for WISDOM in twenty-year-old girls?...

And they say, "Do what you love and the money will follow." NOT TRUE! Me, I love a parade. Now, I'm gonna PARADE out of here because I got a rendezvous with a NAP!

Thank you for your time.

Losers

Listen, the founding fathers said "All men are created equal." The parents of little league children really believe this. Equality at little league means everyone gets a trophy, even me. They must've thought my clumsiness was excellent; they gave me a trophy! Listen, nobody wanted me on their team, and when I asked the coach, "What position should I play?"

The couch said "Any position I put you in, stay away from the ball." I know, I know. This bit isn't very funny, and it's a bit clumsy. But this exactly what you get when you give everybody a trophy. ALL created equal…my ash!

Okay, I call the next bit "Little crumbs." So your living in a very TINY apartment—it's so small, you can't even brush your teeth sideways—where the rents are stable but the tenants ain't, and you look out of your window and see LUXURIOUS penthouse apartments and RITZY people, sipping wine on their beautiful garden terraces. Question: Do you feel bad? NO! Because in your neighbor's apartment, he's looking at a WALL!

Never be ENVIOUS. When I was younger, I wished I was older. Now, I'm living the DREAM, But I'm also living my father's dream. Pop said He didn't become rich and famous on PURPOSE because he knew being "COMPARED" to a rich and famous father would be SUCH a tremendous BURDEN for us kids and he wanted to SPARE us, and you know, in this field of genius, I surpassed my father.

Okay, speaking of marriage, IF you ever find a happily married couple, ALL you have to do is ask "What do you think of your spouse's DRIVING?" Then sit back and enjoy.

The wife says, "It's such a COMFORT when he drives. He flies down the street like he's a fighter pilot. He has to beat the light and the other drivers. I don't need a seat belt; I need a PARACHUTE!"

The husband says, "She doesn't know how to read the road. She drives so slow, she was once passed by a sloth with a CANE. Then she speeds up at a red light!"

But the truth is, my wife and I never fight in the car when there's "company present." When people ask us, "How long was your car trip?" We never describe our trips by time or distance; we just say, "It was a two-fight trip, a three fight trip." It's so DELIGHTFUL!

Speaking of DELIGHTFUL. So you're on a three-lane highway and you're stuck in traffic and you're creeping along at a slow 10 mph, but do you feel bad? NO! Because the other two lanes are STOPPED dead.

Now, there's a little RED car in front of you, and you stay real close to him because if you leave too much of a GAP, someone will cut in front of you. Then, you'll be a WHOLE car length behind. So you continue to ride his bumper. But two minutes later, you notice the OTHER lanes are now going 20 mph. So you decide to change lanes, and you laugh as you pass that little RED car at 20 mph. Then, suddenly, the lane you just moved into stops DEAD! And the lane you just left, not only is it moving, but that little RED car is zipping past you, at TWICE the speed of sound!

An hour later, the traffic clears up and is Zipping along and there's NO signs of an accident, NO roadwork, nothing on the road. SO what happened? I'm stuck in traffic for an hour for NOTHING! That's not fair! Now, I'm pissed. I swear to God, "I'm never, gonna ADOPT a Highway! Hey! Traffic department, here's your trophy!"

So now, I see my EXIT coming up, and I'm off!

The Blank Page

I left this page Blank,…Because I couldn't think of anything
to say,…
But, I wanted to include it,…Before I forgot.

This
Most Deluxe
Blank Space
Is Available
For
ADVERTISING

"I AGREE…CLOTHES, DO MAKE THE MAN!"
(and So, I'll clothes this book with the above cartoon)

Post Scripts

When arguing, be tolerant of the other person's point of view. We are all programmed with different influences... don't RUSH to anger... insisting that YOUR point of view is the only CORRECT view. Is your EGO so fragile?...THAT when Somebody has a different opinion than yours...You immediately go into the DEFEND and ATTACK mode. (In those FEW cases, when your spouse, may NOT be wrong.) In those RARE cases, Calm down, Slow down. Don't make your emotions become your beliefs... Open your eyes.

Niagara Falls, is truly spectacuar,... BOTH from a Worm's Eye view, and a Bird's Eye view.

Don't use "NEVER" and "ALWAYS" in an argument... cause then you're just arguing with the Past... and you're NOT going to solve TODAY's problem.

Carrying around past hurts... Hurts you, and is a HEAVY lift to your happiness.

Remember... Your attitude, will create the road map of your life.

About the Author

It was a dark and stormy night years ago, but during the day, Dom Sileo was a comic book artist for Harvey Publications. They were famous for publishing "Casper the Friendly Ghost" and other cartoon characters. Dom was one of their artists in the '60s and '70s. He drew Richie Rich, the little devil Hotstuff, and Spooky the tough little ghost and an assortment of other characters.

That said, today, one of Dom's big accomplishments is, and he doesn't want to brag (the wife gets so jealous), but he can fold a fitted sheet.

Thank you, thank you very much.

CPSIA information can be obtained
at www.ICGtesting.com
Printed in the USA
LVHW032109260121
677513LV00002B/240